THE GOLDEN YEARS

1952

text: David Sandison

design: Paul Kurzeja

SIENA

A dramatic year by any standard, 1952 mixed tragedy, drama and pathos in equal amounts to become a fascinating period in world history. Tragedy came in the form of the passing of King George VI, of Argentina's charismatic Eva Peron, a woman hated and reviled as much as she was loved and adored, and of Chaim Weizmann, founding father and first President of the infant state of Israel.

Drama came in Senator Richard Nixon's emotional defence of sleaze charges and his survival as running-mate to America's new runaway-victor President Dwight D. Eisenhower, and the bravery of a captain who refused to abandon his ship as January storms smashed it against English rocks.

Pathos came with the publication of the wartime diaries of a Jewish teenager, Anne Frank, who thus became the most famous victim of the Nazi holocaust, and the death sentence passed on a bewildered and retarded Derek Bentley for his complicity in the shooting of a London policeman.

The sporting world gained new heroes - at the

Helsinki Olympic Games, Czechoslovakia's Emil Zatopek smashed records to win three memorable gold medals, and a 17 year old 'Little Mo' Connolly won the first of her Wimbledon tennis titles. Africa became the new hot-spot taking up world headlines. The British clamped down on Kenya's murderous Mau Mau killers and fought a rearguard action against Egyptian police, soldiers and mobs determined to make them leave Suez. And the white South African minority increased its vice-like grip on the now-disenfranchized black majority. Boring? No way!

JAN

East Germany Rejects UN Election Call

The Communist regime in East Germany continued to reinforce their country's determined isolation from the West today when it rejected a United Nations request to supervise free national elections. Last December they turned down an invitation to send a team to this year's Olympics, to be held in Oslo, Norway, because West Germany - a neighbour whose validity they refuse to accept - had accepted an identical invitation from the Olympic Committee.

Courageous Captain Carlsen's Enterprise

A DRAMATIC SEA SAGA which captured international headlines ended today when an American-owned ship, *The Flying Enterprise,* finally sank beneath mountainous waves off the south English coast less than an hour after her captain and a young ship's mate finally abandoned a courageous 12-day vigil aboard the stricken vessel and dived from its almost-submerged funnel to swim ashore.

Captain Henrik Carlsen's memorable adventure began on Christmas Day, shortly after *The Flying Enterprise* left the German port of Hamburg bound for the United States. Hit by hurricane-force winds and huge waves, the ship began to break up.

After managing to get passengers and crew lifted from *The Flying Enterprise* which was by then listing badly enough for her funnel to clip the wavetops, Carlsen was given a tow by a British tug. The two were nearing the safety of the Cornish harbour of Falmouth when his vessel began to sink.

Admitting defeat, Carlsen and the mate leaped to the relative safety of the sea and began their swim towards land. Forty minutes later *The Flying Enterprise* rolled over and sank.

Fine For Death Bus Driver

Controversy in Britain today over the punishment given the driver of a bus which ploughed into a company of Marine cadets in Chatham, Kent on December 4, killing 23 of them.

The man was fined £20 ($60) and banned from driving for three years - way too lenient, according to relatives of those killed and a number of national newspaper columnists.

ARRIVALS
Born this month:
11: Lee Ritenour, US jazz guitarist
23: Robin Zander, US rock musician (Cheap Trick)
29: Tommy Ramone (Thomas Erdelyi), US rock musician (The Ramones)

DEPARTURES
Died this month:
11: Jean-Marie-Gabriel de Lattre de Tassigny, French High Commissioner and Commander-in-Chief French forces in Vietnam. Victor of the January 1951 battle for the North Vietnamese capital Hanoi, his aristocratic manner gained him the affectionate nickname 'King Jean' from his troops.

Ike To Run For US Presidency

General Dwight D. (Ike) Eisenhower, American mastermind supremo of the final defeats of Adolf Hitler and Benito Mussolini in World War II and currently Supreme Allied Commander in Europe, today announced he is prepared to run in the Republican party's primaries to determine their candidate in this year's US presidential elections.

In a cautiously-worded statement issued from his Paris HQ, Ike said that while his military duties meant he would not actually take part in the primaries, he did give his blessing to the campaign launched by leading influential Republicans.

He also confirmed that, while he had never been actively involved in politics, he'd always voted Republican - something advisers to the incumbent Democrat President Harry Truman should have known last November when Truman let it be known that he'd sponsor Ike as a Democratic presidential candidate!

The general already has a formidable opponent to face. The distinguished elder statesman Senator Henry Cabot Lodge has already said he will stand in the Republicans' New Hampshire primary.

Britons Killed As Mobs Rampage In Cairo

Seventeen British people were killed today as mobs of Egyptians rampaged through Cairo in new protests against the UK's continued occupation of the Suez Canal Zone, seized in October 1951 after Egypt's King Farouk demanded a revision of 1936 Anglo-Egyptian treaties and the withdrawal of British forces.

The victims of the murderous mass hysteria were either killed directly by rioters, or burned to death as a number of noted British buildings were set ablaze. These included the very select Turf Club, the world-renowned Shepheard's Hotel, and the Barclays Bank building. The consulate of Lebanon, a friendly Arab nation, was also destroyed as the rioting became uncontrollable.

King Farouk acted swiftly once the full extent of the carnage became clear. Dismissing the government of Nahas Pasha, he declared a dusk-to-dawn curfew with police given shoot-to-kill orders. Already on full alert, British troops in the Canal Zone were boosted on January 27 by the arrival from Cyprus of a squadron of Vampire jets and men of the Scots Guards.

On January 29, 46 Egyptians were killed when British troops over-ran the police station in the town of Ismailia, a key port regained by Egypt in November.

UK-Iran Dispute Grows

The row between Iran and Britain - begun last year when the Iranian government of Prime Minister Mossadegh nationalized the country's oil industry, ordered the seizure of all British petroleum operations and did little to subdue anti-British riots when the UK failed to withdraw staff - worsened this month.

On January 13, the Iranians ordered Britain to close its consulate in the capital, Teheran, effectively cutting off British nationals still in Iran from any source of advice or assistance.

Later, on January 20, Dr. Mossadegh widened the gulf by denouncing the 1857 friendship pact between Britain and Iran.

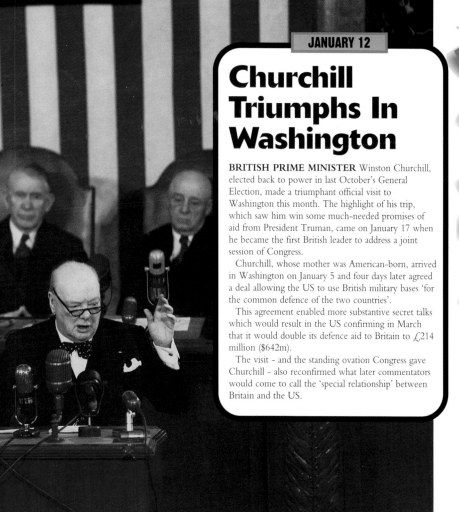

Churchill Triumphs In Washington

BRITISH PRIME MINISTER Winston Churchill, elected back to power in last October's General Election, made a triumphant official visit to Washington this month. The highlight of his trip, which saw him win some much-needed promises of aid from President Truman, came on January 17 when he became the first British leader to address a joint session of Congress.

Churchill, whose mother was American-born, arrived in Washington on January 5 and four days later agreed a deal allowing the US to use British military bases 'for the common defence of the two countries'.

This agreement enabled more substantive secret talks which would result in the US confirming in March that it would double its defence aid to Britain to £214 million ($642m).

The visit - and the standing ovation Congress gave Churchill - also reconfirmed what later commentators would come to call the 'special relationship' between Britain and the US.

Britain And World Mourns Death Of King George

MOST OTHER EVENTS were pushed off the front pages of the world's newspapers today as it was confirmed that King George VI, monarch of the United Kingdom and titular sovereign of the British Commonwealth's many member states, had died peacefully in his sleep at the royal family's Norfolk retreat, Sandringham, on February 6.

Aged 56, the King had apparently made excellent recovery from a September 1951 operation at Buckingham Palace during which doctors removed an infected lung. He and Queen Elizabeth had been at London Airport only six days earlier to send their daughter - who now becomes Queen Elizabeth II - and The Duke of Edinburgh on the first leg of a trip to Kenya, Australia and New Zealand.

It was the Duke who told his wife that she'd become Queen. The two were enjoying a brief safari holiday at The Treetops Hotel, Kenya, when an aide gave him the news and a visibly-shocked Prince Philip hurried to her side. Journalists with the royal couple described her as calm and apparently most concerned that an apology be sent to the people of Australia and New Zealand because she could not now visit them.

While the new monarch and her retinue flew back to London, where she was greeted by Prime Minister Winston Churchill and the Opposition Leader, ex-PM Clement Attlee, an Accession Council had begun work on arrangements for state ceremonies to mark the King's death and make initial preparations for the eventual coronation of the young Queen.

Above all, however, the passing of King George was an occasion for family grief. On February 11 his widow and daughter (both Queens Elizabeth) and his mother, Queen Mary, were the first to pay their respects as his body was laid in state at Westminster Hall.

Two days later the long-exiled Duke of Windsor arrived in London to attend the funeral of a brother who'd only become King because of the Duke's abdication in 1936 to enable his eventual marriage to American divorcee Wallis Simpson.

More than 300,000 people filed past the King's simple oak casket on the day Westminster Hall was opened to the public. On February 15 the funeral began when the coffin was placed on a gun carriage and men of the Household Cavalry marched it in slow time to the royal train at Paddington station, where members of world royal families and political leaders waited to accompany it to Windsor Castle. It was there, in the ancestral vault of St. George's Chapel, that the body of King George - a shy man who'd been unwillingly thrust into the spotlight but had proved an inspirational and courageous figurehead during the war - was finally laid to rest.

A new Elizabethan Age had begun.

UN Meets In New York Home

One of the United Nations' greatest problems - the international forum never had a permanent place to call its own and had been forced to constantly relocate to makeshift bases, including London, Geneva and Paris - was solved today.

The first session in the UN's new custom-built New York headquarters was held today, with delegates reportedly delighted at the ultra-modern facilities installed. The building, a gift from the US government, is to cost the UN only a peppercorn rent even though it occupies a hefty slice of Manhattan waterfront real estate worth millions.

NEWS IN BRIEF

2: Armed Argentinians forced a British party to return to their ship when they attempted to disembark on the disputed Antarctic territory of Graham Land

3: In continuing peace talks, Communists agreed that all North Korean prisoners released by the Allies would not fight again

4: In London, the government offered UK farmers £5 ($15) for every acre of grassland they ploughed for crop-growing

17: West Germany's application for NATO membership put off in Paris by the US, Britain and France

21: In Britain, ID cards introduced during WWII were abolished

FEBRUARY 26

Churchill Admits British A-Bomb Secret

PRIME MINISTER Winston Churchill admitted in the House of Commons today that Britain has become the third member of the nuclear club, until now consisting only of the United States and Russia.

While confirming the UK had developed an atomic bomb and has a plant capable of producing more, he attacked the Labour government of Clement Attlee which had initiated the research programme while all the time denouncing atomic weapons. The project was so secret, he had known nothing of it until he was re-elected Prime Minister in October last year, claimed Churchill.

The British bomb will be tested later this year in Australia, the PM said. A Downing Street statement stressed that the test would be carried out in conditions which would ensure no radioactivity risk to people or animals.

The British news was welcomed by Connecticut's Senator McMahon, chairman of the US Senate's Atomic Energy Committee. He said the UK's nuclear capability would aid world peace 'because it will add to the free world's total deterring power'.

FEBRUARY 26

Malayan Hostilities Continue

Casualty figures in British forces' year-long battle against Communist guerrillas in the Malayan jungles continued to mount this month. On February 17, seven soldiers of the Gordon Highlanders regiment were killed by insurgents. British response was swift and deadly: five days later 22 Communists were reported dead after a two-day sweep operation through suspected regions.

FEBRUARY 21

Fans Besiege Wilding-Taylor Wedding

More than 1,000 screaming fans halted traffic around London's Caxton Hall registry office today to disrupt the supposedly-secret wedding of English screen star Michael Wilding to the young British-born, American-based actress Elizabeth Taylor (pictured together right). There's a big age gap between the two. Wilding, whose current hit is the war drama Into The Blue, is 40, while his violet-eyed bride is only 19. The young Miss Taylor, who was evacuated to the US during the war and became a child star via such films as National Velvet and Little Women, is currently enjoying a huge success with her latest movie A Place In The Sun. Those who think she's maybe too young to be marrying should know she's been a Mrs once before. In 1950 she promised to love, cherish and obey hotel chain millionaire Conrad Hilton 'til death (or a great divorce settlement) did them part!

FEB

MAR

US Doctors Use First Artificial Heart In Op

A MECHANICAL HEART HAS been used successfully to maintain a patient's blood flow during an operation, according to a statement made today by officials of the Pennsylvania Hospital in Philadelphia.

Although the patient - 41 years old steelworker Peter During - died later, his death was said to be from causes not related to the use of the artificial heart. That had enabled the team of nine doctors, two technicians and five nurses to carry out an 80-minute investigation to establish what was restricting the normal flow of blood from his natural heart.

The Philadelphia story is a triumphant breakthrough for medical science. It is known that experiments to develop a bypass device are being carried out at most of the world's research hospitals, and the US team's success will have a positive impact on the kind of corrective surgery this and future generations of physicians can now attempt.

South African Crisis

The South African parliament was thrown into chaos today when Prime Minister Dr DF Malan - a noted hardliner when it comes to restricting the civil rights of non-whites - said he would not accept a Supreme Court judgement declaring illegal a recently-passed law to remove Coloured (mixed race) voters from the electoral register.

The court's ruling said the Afrikaner Nationalist Party's law, which was introduced to worldwide condemnation in May 1951, was invalid because such a fundamental change to South Africa's constitution required a two-thirds parliamentary majority.

A defiant Dr Malan is determined to have his way, however, and his government's increasingly racist stance will set South Africa on a long and bloody collision course both in and outside its borders.

US Rejects China's Germ Warfare Claim

While talks to reconcile still-outstanding differences between the two sides in the Korean War apparently proceed slowly but positively. the Chinese communist regime of Mao Tse-tung appears unable - or unwilling - to pass up any excuse to muddy the waters.

Today's attempt was a claim that the US is using germ warfare in the Chinese province of Manchuria which borders North Korea. The allegation has been vehemently denied by Washington.

Chinese hopes of international support are not aided by their refusal to allow independent observers into Manchuria to view evidence they say exists to support their claims.

Kelly Causes A Big Splash

The all-singin', all-dancin' Gene Kelly has a smash on his hands. His newest movie *Singin' In The Rain* is breaking box-office records in the US and Britain this month. Critics have been doing somersaults in praise of this brilliant comic tribute to the time when sound arrived to transform Hollywood.

Starring with Kelly, who stops the show with a fantastic title song dance sequence in a torrential downpour, are sidekick Donald O'Connor, love interest Debbie Reynolds and Jean Hagen as the silent movie sex-goddess whose career crashes when microphones reveal her corncrake Bronx shriek.

ARRIVALS
Born this month:
2: Gary Grainger, UK rock musician (Strider)
7: William Boyd, British novelist, screenwriter; Vivian Richards, West Indian cricketer (*see Came and Went pages*)
9: Bill Beaumont, English rugby player, TV commentator
18: Pat Eddery, UK jockey
23: Dave Bortram, UK rock musician/singer (Showaddywaddy)
24: Robert Fox, UK theatrical producer

DEPARTURES
Died this month:
15: Nevil Vincent Sidgwick, British chemist

3: In House of Commons, Labour Party split as 57 left-wing Bevan supporters defied a three-line whip in a defence vote

11: In the Budget, Chancellor Rab Butler raised taxes on profits, increased tax allowances and raised bank rate to 4 per cent

22: Forty-four killed in Frankfurt, Germany when a Dutch KLM plane crashed while trying to land in fog and rain; Over 200 reported dead and 2,500 injured as a tornado swept through mid-western USA

25: British doctors are awarded a £500 ($1500) p.a. rise, backdated to 1948

MARCH 21

Nkrumah Becomes First African Prime Minister

A LANDMARK DAY for Africa as Dr Kwame Nkrumah became the first black politician to be democratically elected a national prime minister when his party won the Gold Coast's first general election. Setting a trend which would become the norm among many African leaders, Dr Nkrumah was serving a prison sentence for treason when elected.

Also in common with other future prime ministers and presidents, Dr Nkrumah spent many years working and studying abroad - in is case in Britain and the US - before returning home to become a thorn in the existing colonial power's side.

The new PM entered Gold Coast politics in 1948, founded *The Daily Mail* newspaper and used its pages to attack the old regime. Eventually going too far, he was arrested, tried for sedition and imprisoned, events which only helped him win the election.

There is some doubt about Kwame (which means Saturday, the day his mother said he was born) Nkrumah's real age. The only definite fix to establish that is the fact he was three years old when a cargo ship was grounded near his remote coastal village home. Records show that occurred in 1913, so that would make him 42 now.

MARCH 29

Oxford Steer Through Blizzard

Last year it was high waves which sank the Oxford team in the annual University Boat Race, which Cambridge won when it was re-rowed a week later.

This year's contest was staged in the heart of a blizzard, and while thousands did brave the weather to watch from the banks of the River Thames, visbility was so bad that most of them had to be told that Oxford had avenged their defeat.

Democracy Knocked Back In Cuba & Africa

Not a good month for elected representatives in Africa or the island of Cuba.

On March 2, King Farouk attempted to assume control over the increasingly chaotic mess the Egyptian parliament had become in the wake of the Suez Canal Zone crisis and ordered its suspension for a month.

He will run his country's fight with Britain without interference from inter-party wrangling.

On March 10, Cuba found itself with a new self-appointed leader when General Fulgencio Batista - who'd run the island state as a dictatorship between 1933 and 1944, when elections forced him to hand over to President Carlos Socarras - decided he'd seen enough of democracy to know it didn't work and ousted Socarras in a military-backed coup.

And on March 25, French authorities in the North African country of Tunisia grew weary of anti-colonial disturbances and arrested Prime Minister Hamed Shenik. The move sparked off greater resistance to French rule and led to the eventual offer, in 1954, of Tunisian autonomy and eventual independence.

OSCARS BECOME THE WORLD'S GREATEST SHOW

It had to happen. As the film industry's most deadly enemy - the ever-present television - gained a hold as an increasingly-powerful news and entertainment medium, it was inevitable that movieland's annual beanfest would appear, in all its tacky wonder, on the world's smaller screens.

Ironically, the fact that the 1952 Academy Awards bash was the first to be televized was due entirely to the three biggest film studios: Warner Bros, Columbia and Universal. When they said they didn't want to fund the Oscars any more, NBC made an offer The Academy of Motion Pictures Arts and Sciences couldn't refuse.

Movie buffs who tuned in to watch the nerve-wracking process, catch a close-up glimpse of their idols and share the triumphs and disappointments of the evening, witnessed one of those Hollywood occasions when it's obvious that studio politics have muddied the waters.

What happened to *Singin' In The Rain,* for instance? One of the biggest international box-office hits of 1951-52, it failed to make the Best Picture shortlist. Director and leading man Gene Kelly was not nominated as either Best Actor or Best Director, while his superb stooge Donald O'Connor didn't win a nomination as Supporting Actor.

Only Jean Hagan, whose brilliant portrayal of the silent screen goddess whose career ends when the arrival of sound revealed a corncrake Bronx shrieking voice, was nominated as Supporting Actress, but she had to give way to the magnificent Gloria Grahame (for *The Bad And The Beautiful*).

More strangely, perhaps, Cecil B. DeMille's circus extravaganza *The Greatest Show On Earth* won the Best Picture prize. No-one else involved in this dinosaur, except the three-man team who won Oscars for their storyline, was even nominated for major awards.

Those went to Gary Cooper (Best Actor, for *High Noon*), Shirley Booth (Best Actress, for *Come Back,Little Sheba*), Anthony Quinn (Supporting Actor, for *Viva Zapata!*) and John Ford (Best Director, for *The Quiet Man*).

It's High Noon, and
Gary shows Grace what
a man's gotta do

Other anomalies which probably puzzled couch potatoes: Marlon Brando failed, for the second year running, to win the Best Actor award for *Viva Zapata!*, and John Wayne didn't even get a mention for his career-best performance in *The Quiet Man*.

There were some interesting signs of life from the British film industry, though. The quirky comedy *The Lavender Hill Mob* won a Story and Screenplay Oscar for T E B Clark, lead man Alec Guinness was nominated as Best Actor, while newcomer Richard Burton was shortlisted in the Supporting Actor category for his part in *My Cousin Rachel*.

Almost unnoticed (as the technical awards usually are), the Oscar for Best Sound was won by the London Film Sound Department for the documentary short *Breaking The Sound Barrier*.

APRIL

APRIL 10

Ike's Presidential Bid Gains Momentum

HE MAY BE A RELUCTANT bridegroom, but as the campaign to get General Dwight D Eisenhower nominated as their presidential candidate at this year's Republican Party convention picks up speed and support, there were signs this month that Ike was beginning to take his chances of success seriously.

On April 10, the man who said in January that his duties as Supreme Commander of NATO forces in Europe took precedence over presidential primary canvassing, officially asked President Harry Truman to relieve him from the post on June 1.

Two days later, when news of his request became public knowledge and he was pressed for a statement, Eisenhower confirmed that he would resign from the US Army if the Republicans did make him their candidate. Ike was the natural focus of attention in Paris on April 16 when NATO's new headquarters were officially opened at the Palais de Chaillot, but restricted his comments to compliments about the building he was about to leave - for, on April 28 it was announced that the US/UN Korean War supremo General Matthew Ridgway had been appointed as his successor.

APRIL 21

Labour Loses Cripps

Britain's Labour Party lost one of its most distinguished elders today with the death of Sir Stafford Cripps. Aged 63, he had often proved a thorn in Labour's side, even being expelled in 1939 for public disagreement with party leaders.

An able and even-handed diplomat, Cripps became the British wartime government's special envoy to India in 1942. It was he who began the long and tortuous process of negotiating Indian independence with Gandhi, a lengthy process he continued after the war as a member of the Labour government.

Appointed Minister of Economic Affairs in 1947, he was the Chancellor of the Exchequer who devalued the pound by 30 per cent against the dollar in 1949 to spark a flurry of other currencies' devaluations.

Nicknamed The Iron Chancellor, Cripps was finally forced to resign in October 1950 as his health declined. A committed vegetarian and advocate of austerity in all things, he'd managed the British economy through some of its hardest times.

Official: Pacific War Is Over

Almost eight years after the last shots were fired, and eight months after world diplomats concluded a final wording agreeable to almost 50 governments - except the Soviet Union - the peace treaty to formalize the end of the war with Japan was finally signed today by President Harry Truman (pictured left) in a brief White House ceremony.

The treaty, which the other 49 countries will co-sign, recognizes Japanese sovereignty and enables the wartime enemy to begin governing itself again from April 1953.

Russia's beef with the treaty concerns an agreement allowing the US to continue operating naval and military bases in Japan - a move the Soviet Union says confirms America's warlike and expansionist intentions in the Pacific region.

President Truman used the occasion to sign security treaties with Australia and New Zealand, as well as a mutual defence pact with The Philippines.

ARRIVALS

Born this month:
4: Dave Hill, UK rock musician (Slade)
7: Bruce Gary, US rock musician (The Knack)
14: Jerry Knight, US rock musician (Raydio)
23: Narada Michael Walden, US jazz/rock musician

DEPARTURES

Died this month:
1: Ferec Molnár, Hungarian playwright
21: Sir Richard Stafford Cripps, British lawyer, diplomat, statesman *(see main story)*
23: Elisabeth Schumann, US opera singer
25: Gertie Millar, Countess of Dudley, former musical comedy actress

3: Although losers in the general election, Labour won 55 seats and control of London County Council today

5: At Aintree Racecourse, Liverpool, Mr. H. Lane's Teal won The Grand National

9: Attempting to aid recession-hit British textile manufacturers, the government announced it will place £20m orders with the worst-affected

24: In Nuremburg, Germany, a tribunal began hearings on the Katyn Forest massacre of 1940

30: Matching international practice, the UK pharmaceutical industry switched its weights and measures to the metric system

APRIL 25

French Launch Huge Vietnam Offensive

THE DENSELY-FORESTED HILL country near Tay Minh, site of the North Vietnamese communist Viet Minh army's military and political headquarters in South Vietnam, was the scene of fierce battles today as French forces launched a massive attack designed to smash their enemy's strategic power base.

More than 6,000 men were involved in the offensive, only some 75 miles north-west of the South Vietnamese capital, Saigon. The attack came as French government officials voiced concern at what they percieve as increased Chinese involvement in Viet Minh leader Ho Chi Minh's bid to over-run the country.

If the communists win the battle for Indo-China, all southern Asia would be easy prey, said Jean le Tourneau, the French Minister Resident in Indo-China.

He warned that France would ask for United Nations intervention if China physically entered the war. At present, their involvement appears to be confined to giving the Viet Minh huge amounts of arms and other supplies, along with the USSR.

Britian Offers Sudan Self Rule

The British government tried to head off King Farouk's bid to merge Sudan with Egypt today when it offered Sudan a type of limited self-rule.

It was a bold move which, while it would remove one of Farouk's best cards and increase pressure on him to compromise in the struggle to control the Suez Canal Zone, would eventually rebound on Britain.

When a general election was finally held in Sudan in November 1953, the pro-Egyptian National Unionist Party would form the first government.

US Bomb Tests On TV

In a public relations exercise designed to keep the American public firmly on the side of the US Atomic Energy Commission's H-bomb test programme, the latest in a series of explosions in the Nevada desert was shown live on network TV today, and attracted an audience of more than 35 million concerned tax-payers. The new tests were announced on April 1, and the government used the spotlight on all things atomic to unveil the USAF's latest weapon, the huge 8-engined YB-60 jet bomber, on April 5.

MAY 16

British Parliament Votes For Equal Pay

IN THE HOUSE OF COMMONS, British politicians gave a boost to the principle of equal pay for women when they passed a government bill to introduce such pay structures.

Introducing the measure, Financial Secretary to the Treasury John Boyd-Carpenter said that while the government would only enforce the ruling 'in stages', they planned to start with the Civil Service to ensure that women doing the same jobs as men would be paid the same.

Although the Labour opposition voted for the bill, they pressed the Conservatives for a more definite date. With a growing and increasingly-vocal equal-pay lobby staging rallies in many leading cities, Labour could argue that Britain's women were not prepared to wait much longer.

These probably included the women teachers the last Labour government awarded a pay rise in October 1950. While male teachers' salaries rose to £630 ($1800) a year, their female counterparts were increased to only £504!

MAY 5

'New' Anthem For Germany

To many survivors and veterans of World War II, the choice of words and music for the new West German national anthem is important. There are just too many bad memories of Adolf Hitler's Third Reich involved in the traditional *Deutschland Uber Alles*. Critics and cynics had their worst fears realized today when the Bonn government opted for a compromise. The old anthem would stay, but without its first two gung-ho verses. Quite simply, no-one had come up with a new alternative anyone liked.

MAY 1

TWA Start Price War

With BOAC about to steal a march with its introduction of jet travel tomorrow *(see main story)*, the American-owned Trans World Airlines tried to hijack its thunder today by launching its lower-cost Tourist Class throughout its international fleet of turbo-prop airliners.

It's a bold move which involved extensive (and expensive) refurbishment and alterations to TWA planes, but one which led to similar moves by nine other airlines determined to compete in the ever-growing market for international travel.

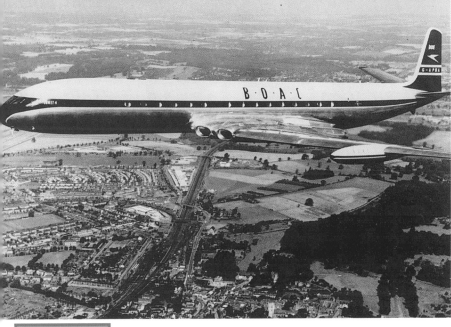

3: English soccer books re-written as Newcastle United beat Arsenal 1-0 in the FA Cup Final, the first team to win in successive years since 1891

9: More local government election gains for Labour Party, which now controls 21 British councils

10: At Cannes Film Festival, Orson Welles' *Othello* awarded a Grand Prix

20: Eight new nature reserves in Scotland and England were announced today by the Nature Conservancy Council

29: South African crisis deepened as MPs voted to allow PM Malan to reject last month's High Court ruling

MAY 2

Comet Introduces Jet Travel

The sci-fi dream of jet travel became reality today when 36 passengers boarded a British Overseas Airways Corporation (BOAC) Comet airliner for the first scheduled flight between London and South Africa's Johannesburg Airport.

The flight was seen off by hundreds of spectators who packed public enclosures and the windows of office blocks to cheer and wave as the Comet began its 6,700 mile journey.

Non-stop longhaul flights were still a thing of the future, however. The Comet made stops at Rome (Italy), Beirut (Lebanon), Khartoum (Sudan), Entebbe (Uganda) and Livingston (Northern Rhodesia) before arriving at Johannesburg 18 hours 40 minutes later.

ARRIVALS

Born this month:
3: Alan Wells, Scottish and Olympic 100 metres champion
9: Patrick Ryecart, UK actor
14: David Byrne, UK/US rock musician, songwriter, producer (Talking Heads)
18: George Strait, US country music singer, songwriter
19: Grace Jones, Jamaican/US model, singer, actress;
Joey Ramone, US rock musician (The Ramones)
25: David Jenkins, UK athlete

DEPARTURES

Died this month:
1: William Fox (Wilhelm Fried), US film producer
6: Maria Montessori, Italian physician and educationalist
(see main story)

MAY 6

Pioneer Montessori Dies

Dr Maria Montessori, a world pioneer in the field of nursery education, died today in Holland. She was 81.

Italy's first-ever registered woman physician, Dr Montessori initially specialized in work with brain-damaged children. In 1907 she opened her first school in Rome, drawing on that experience to encourage spontaneity and self-discovery among able infants.

Although her fame and methods spread internationally, they fell from favour as other theories became popular. It was not until the early sixties that Montessori schools, all emphasizing early reading and writing, once again returned to prominence.

MAY 5

New Nation For Africa?

The first moves to create a new federation of the three British-ruled countries of Northern Rhodesia, Southern Rhodesia and Nyasaland were agreed in principle today in London.

If the union does go ahead - and there are many black African voices raised in protest even though the British government says their rights and interests will be paramount as talks begin - central Africa would have a new nation of more than seven million people.

MAY 8

Allies Bomb N. Koreans To Speed Up Talks

EXASPERATED BY the delaying tactics of communist delegates to the peace talks in Korea, UN commander General Matthew Ridgway delivered a 'final' warning today when Allied fighter bombers smashed the city of Suan in a dawn-to-dusk raid.

The historic town and strategic supply centre was decimated by bombs and napalm, after which it was strafed by a barrage of machine-gun and cannon fire.

Besides impressing the North Koreans that the UN would not put up with their continued refusal to reach a final agreement, Ridgway also ensured they would not be able to mount a large-scale offensive using supplies stored in Suan.

The raid was one of General Ridgway's last acts before leaving the Korean arena to fly to Paris where, on May 30, he took over from General Eisenhower as NATO chief. His successor in Korea was General Mark Clark.

New Korean Tensions

Any optimism that the continuing talks in Kaesong would bring a speedy end to the Korean War receded this month with three key events.

On June 3, US troops stormed a prisoner of war camp on the island of Koje when North Koreans staged an open rebellion against their captors. Thirty prisoners were killed before the mutiny was quelled.

China's intentions became clear on June 8 when intelligence reports confirmed that more than 100,000 Chinese reinforcements were on their way to positions behind the ceasefire zone.

And on June 23, UN planes were sent in to damage North Korea's infrastructure severely by bombing hydro-electric plants serving a number of strategically important towns known to have arms manufacturing bases.

JUNE 15

Anne Frank's Holocaust Diary Published

ONE OF THE MOST MOVING chronicles of World War II appeared in world bookstores today with the publication of *The Diary of Anne Frank* , the notes of a German Jewish teenager who spent two years hiding with her family from Hitler's SS in Amsterdam before they were discovered and sent to their deaths in concentration camps.

Anne (pictured left) was just 13 when she began keeping her diary in 1942. Her account of the time she, her parents and five siblings lived in the claustrophobic secret hideaway in her father's business premises, would prove one of the publishing sensations of the decade.

A full and honest account of the pressures such an existence has on people, Anne became philosophical as time went on. "I have now reached the stage where I don't care if I live or die", she wrote, shortly before the family were captured in July 1944. Anne's father was the only one to survive, and he managed to hold on to her diary through the horrors of The Final Solution.

JUNE 4

Ike Begins His Campaign

Dwight D Eisenhower, back in the United States after resigning as Supreme Commander of NATO, began his campaign to win the Republican Party nomination as presidential candidate today with his first public speech.

Ike set out his stall, and his agenda for the entire campaign, by attacking one-party states and promising to steer the US to a period of increased prosperity and stability.

While observers rated the speech only middling in content and style, the standing ovation it won from party workers only confirmed Ike's front-runner status in the Republicans' forthcoming Chicago convention.

JUNE 26

Congress Ignores Truman's Veto

Congress delivered a slap to President Truman today when it voted to over-ride his veto of the controversial McCarren-Walter Bill which will apply severe immigration quotas he described as discriminatory and unworthy of a nation founded on the ideal of welcoming immigrants.

The confrontation was inevitable, given popular opinion that the United States can ill afford to allow unrestricted access to a workplace still struggling to rebuild itself from the ravages of WWII.

NEWS IN BRIEF

8: In London, William Dickson appointed to succeed Sir John Slessor as Chief of the Air Staff in January 1953

14: USS Nautilus, the world's first atomic powered submarine, launched at a ceremony attended by President Truman; Andrei Gromyko appointed Soviet ambassador to Britain

16: In Europe, the Schuman Plan to create a steel and coal community was ratified by France, Germany, Italy, Belgium and Holland

29: Disaster for Royal Air Force as the prototype of new jet fighter, the delta wing Gloster GA-5, crashed and exploded during tests

JUNE 1

Soviets Move To Isolate West Berlin

THE PEOPLE OF WEST BERLIN AWOKE this morning to the reality of isolation from families and friends in the communist controlled eastern part of their city, which has been stranded deep inside the Soviet Zone since the end of World War II.

From midnight, all West Germans will need special permits to enter the Eastern Zone. And while this movement ban does not apply to Berlin's road and rail links to the West, it effectively cuts West Berliners off from half the old capital and all surrounding countryside.

Ominously, the Soviets have set up a three-mile security belt to enforce the new restrictions - including a 10-yard wide strip within which Russian and East German frontier guards have been given 'shoot on sight' orders.

JUNE 17

New UK Sports Records

Two triumphs made British hearts fill with pride this month - one in the very English sport of cricket, the other in the ever-competitive athletics arena.

Already a hero to schoolboy followers of the summer game, the Middlesex batsman Denis Compton passed the notable milestone of his hundredth first-class 100 runs on June 11 when he scored 107 in his county's game against Kent at the world cricket HQ of Lord's in North London.

A day later, Britain claimed a new world record when Chris Chataway (pictured right) raced to cover two miles of track in 8 mins 55.6 seconds.

Protests Rock South Africa

Outrage among South Africa's Cape Coloured and Indian communities at the government's decision to strip them of voting rights became open confrontation today when hundreds of protestors singing 'God Save Africa' crossed segregation barriers to defy the law requiring them to carry official passes.

It was the first mass protest of what its organizers, who announced their intentions on June 1, have stressed is a non-violent campaign against the country's growing apartheid laws.

Some 150 people - including blacks, most of whom were wearing the distinctive gold, green and black armbands of The African National Congress party - were arrested when they handed themselves over to police and refused to apply for bail.

JUNE

OFFY-KURTIS DOMINATES INDY 500

The US motor racing scene witnessed a revolution in 1951 when the so-called Offy-Kurtis car (fuel-injected, four-cylinder engines built by the Offenhauser team, lightweight chassis developed by Frank Kurtis) of Lee Wallard became the first to tear round the Indianapolis 500 track in less than three hours - two hours and 57 minutes, and an average speed of 126.244 mph.

Wallard was not on the starting grid for the 1952 Indy 500. He'd been tragically killed four days after his 1951 victory in a sprint event. But there were 29 Offy-powered machines, 20 of them with Kurtis bodies, among the 33 starters. You couldn't get odds on an Offy-Kurtis victory.

As it was, the more traditional car of 22-year-old Troy Ruttman emerged as the last lap winner, with his machine inspiring the description 'roadster' and changing the face of US racing for years to come.

Bill Vukovich's Offy-Kurtis KK500A took an early lead, but it was the Cummins Diesel Special of Fred Agabashian which overhauled him. In Lap 71 disaster struck when Agabashian's supercharger developed problems and Vukovich regained the lead, with Ruttman hot on his heels.

When Vukovich hit and slid along a wall in the last lap, it allowed Ruttman - at that point 19 seconds behind - to coast home for a notable against-all-odds win.

GOAL DIFFERENCE WINS FOR ARSENAL AND RANGERS

Both the English and Scottish football league championships were won by the narrowest of margins - goal difference - this year.

In England, Arsenal won the title, despite sharing the same 54 points end-of-season total as Preston North End.

They were less fortunate in the FA Cup Final, a victory which would have given them the much-coveted double. They met an on-song Newcastle United, who beat them 2-0 to rack up their second Cup win in succession.

In Scotland, Hibernian's hopes of a third successive league championship were denied when, despite sharing points honours of 43 with Rangers, a count-back of goals gave the Glasgow team the title.

The Scottish League Cup Final saw a rampant Motherwell overwhelm Dundee to emerge 4-0 winners. The national side, 1-0 losers to England in their annual home championship meeting, enjoyed a moral victory when they hammered a touring US side (who'd helped knock England out of the 1950 World Cup) by a massive 6-0 at Hamden Park.

LIONS' ROAR STOPS BROWNS

The Cleveland Browns, in their third successive championship title game since joining the NFL in 1950,

were over-run by the Detroit Lions, who emerged 17-7 winners - the second of an eventual four championships to be won by the Motor City's machine.

It was a notable poaching season for the LA Rams' Dick 'Night Train' Lane. He notched up 14 interceptions during the season to set a new record.

ENGLISH CRICKET GOES PRO

Finally bowing to the inevitable, the English test selectors appointed a professional cricketer to the national captaincy for the 1952 summer series against the Indian tourists.

The man chosen to end the nonsensical tradition of Gentlemen and Players was the brilliant Len Hutton, a member of the Freddie Brown-led England team which had drawn the recent winter test series in India 1-1-3.

His arrival, and leadership, was inspired and England won the subsequent series 3-1.

South Africa's cricketers were also inspired this year. In December they beat Australia for the first time in 42 years. Their star turn was bowler Hugh Tayfield, who had a purple patch spell of three wickets in nine maiden overs.

JULY

Argentina's Shirtless Ones Mourn Evita

A REMARKABLE CHAPTER in the history of Argentina came to a close today with the death of Eva Peron, wife of President Juan Peron. Loved by Argentina's *descamisados,* or 'shirtless poor', as deeply as she was hated by those who only saw the widespread corruption and police state excesses of the Peron regime, Evita was only 33 when she died of ovarian cancer.

The news broke at 9.42 tonight when an announcer broke into a radio programme to say: 'Our spiritual leader has gone!' Within minutes the streets of Buenos Aires were filled as weeping supporters flooded towards the presidential palace.

The illegitimate daughter of a cook, Maria Eva Ibarguren was a 15 year old nightclub singer when she met Juan Peron, then Minister of Labour. Married less than a year later, the popular and charismatic Evita soon became a formidable helpmate in her husband's rise to the presidency.

In 1945, when he was arrested on treason charges, Evita won Peron's release by broadcasting radio summons for her worker-followers to rise up and free him. The ruling junta let him go rather than face a revolution.

A formidable champion of women's rights, Evita successfully fought to give Argentina's women the vote and legalized divorce. The dark side of her nature showed in the merciless way she treated all who questioned the Peron presidency - disappearances and torture were widespread.

A brief life may have ended, but a legend was about to begin.

Last Tram To New Cross

The shape of London's transport changed forever today when the capital's last-ever tram left its depot in Woolwich and set off through Greenwich for its final destination in New Cross. Thousands of Londoners watched nostalgically as hundreds struggled to board or grab a ride on this piece of history which transportation experts ruled outdated and too expensive to modernize. New buses and improved track-free roads will be more than capable of handling future traffic demands, they promise.

British Census Reveals Changes

The preliminary findings of Britain's 1951 national census were released today and showed some dramatic changes in the way its citizens live.

Living longer, marrying earlier, divorcing more often and moving away from traditional manufacturing jobs, Britons are also becoming more solitary: some 1.5 million now live alone, twice the number who did so in 1931, the last year a full census was conducted. Living conditions remain generally poor. One in twenty households still have no piped water supply, while one in three lack a bath!

Power See-Saw As Iranians Riot

The struggle for power in Iran took more twists this month as the country continued to try to wrest control of its oil industry from Britain.

On July 17, the Shah replaced the hardline anti-British Prime Minister Dr Mossadegh with the less acerbic Ahmad Ghavam. The capital Teheran was immediately hit by anti-Ghavam riots and the Shah was forced to re-appoint Mossadegh only five days later.

His hand reinforced by public opinion, Dr Mossadegh was able to demand and assume emergency powers from the Shah on July 31, leaving him free to get even tougher with the Anglo-Iranian Oil Company and subdue his opponents.

JULY 5

Little Mo Wins First Wimbledon Title

Maureen Connolly, the 17 year old American tennis star her fans call 'Little Mo', today became the youngest Wimbledon All-England Ladies champion since 15 year old Lottie Dod beat all-comers in 1887. It was her first appearance in the tournament.

Her opponent was the formidable Louise Brough, three times winner since the war and making her fifth finals appearance. Her past success and greater experience proved no match for Little Mo's youthful energy and superb backhand.

Although she led 5-4 in the first set, Brough was held to three deuces before the young Californian took the set 7-5, and powered through to win the second 6-3.

The men's title was won by Australian Frank Sedgman, who beat the Egypt-based Czech defector Jaroslav Drobny to avenge his 1950 final defeat by American J . Patty.

JULY 7

Blue Riband For America

The much-coveted Blue Riband title for the fastest crossing of the Atlantic between Britain and America has long been the subject of friendly rivalry between the passenger liner operators of both countries, with a lot of pride at stake for the captain and crew who break the existing record - and some handy public relations for their employers.

So champagne celebrations were the order of the day for the master and officers of the US liner *United States* today as they took the Blue Riband back from the British-owned Cunard liner *Queen Mary*. They had completed the New York-Southampton run in only three days, 10 hours and 40 minutes.

Farouk Ousted By Egyptian Coup

KING FAROUK, the ruler of Egypt with an international reputation as a womanizing playboy *(pictured with Irma Minutolo, 'Miss Naples')* and gambler, was stripped of his powers today in a coup led by army commander General Mohammed Neguib.

The coup followed the King's repeated refusal to fire personal favourites implicated in profiting from the sale of defective weapons to an Egyptian army fighting to eject British forces from the Suez Canal Zone. Already unpopular, especially with devout Muslims who found his lifestyle offensive, Farouk had finally pushed his opponents too far.

Civil unrest following the July 1 appointment of Hussein Sirry Pasha as Prime Minister grew so bad a state of alert was proclaimed in Cairo only three days later. Within days of the coup, Farouk abdicated in favour of his 9 month old son and sailed out of Alexandria aboard a luxury yacht, *en route* to one of his Mediterranean homes. The new regime ensured the infant prince would never succeed his father when they abolished the traditional heriditary titles of Pasha and Bey on July 31.

JULY

Three Gold Record-Breaking Wins For Zatopek In Olympics

HELSINKI, FINLAND: The 1952 Olympic Games belonged to one very special athlete - Czechoslovakia's 29 year old Emil Zatopek. At the Games to defend the 10,000 metre title he'd won at the 1948 London Olympics - something most experts believed he'd do, despite a strong field - Zatopek astonished everyone by announcing he'd also compete in the 5,000 metres and the marathon!

A quick check of timetables confirmed his insanity. If Zatopek did run in the two track finals, he'd only have three days to recover before tackling the gruelling 25-plus miles of the marathon for the first time in his life.

If it was madness, it turned out to be the inspired kind.

Zatopek didn't exactly stroll through the 10,000 metres to regain his title and win the Gold medal - he set a new Olympic record of 29 mins 17 secs, finishing 15 seconds ahead of silver medallist, Frenchman Alain Mimoun and 31 ahead of Russia's bronze winner, Aleksander Anufriyev.

The 5000 metre final was a lot closer. Zatopek found himself up against Mimoun once more, as well as Britain's Christopher Chataway and West Germany's Herbert Schade. All three looked as if they were running backwards at the final bend as Zatopek kicked, and roared past them all (Chataway falling in the process) to take his second Gold - and his second Olympic record - with a 14 mins 06.6 secs time.

The Czech's marathon victory, which was also achieved in a new Olympic record time of 2 hrs 23 mins 03.2 secs, was all the more remarkable for it having been his debut. Zatopek was characteristically modest about having beaten Argentinia's Reinaldo Gorno by more than a minute and a half, and typically dismissive of the marathon itself. It was, he pronounced, 'very boring'!

The Czech people in general, and the Zatopek family in particular, had a fourth reason to celebrate by the end of the Helsinki Games. Emil's wife Dana also won a Gold medal and set a new Olympic record when she threw her javelin a mighty 50.47 metres, to make the Zatopeks the only husband and wife team ever to win events in the same Games.

Foxhunter Saves Britain's Blushes

Showjumping genius Foxhunter, ridden by Colonel Harry Llewellyn, saved Britain from the ignominy of a Gold Medal-free Olympics when he jumped a clear round to win his team the Prix des Nations title and the Brits their sole Gold.

It was, as the Duke of Wellington said after the Battle of Waterloo, 'a damn close-run thing'. The show-jumping was the final event of the 1952 Olympics, and 15 minutes after the hurdles and gates had been cleared from the great Helsinki stadium, the closing ceremony began.

Ingy's Boxing Shame

There was no Silver medal won in the 1952 Olympic heavyweight boxing tournament. In one of the most shameful and shaming decisions in the history of the Games, Sweden's Ingemar Johansson was disqualified in the second round of his final fight with American Hayes Edward Sanders.

Apparently determined to do anything but make a proper fight of it, Johanssen - who would go on to a long and successful professional career - was adjudged to be guilty of 'passivity' and ordered from the ring.

Strangely, South Africa's bronze medallist Andries Nieman was not promoted to take silver. That remains in the record books as un-awarded.

Schoolboy Is New King Of Jordan

The constitutional crisis which has faced the Middle East nation of Jordan since the assassination of King Abdullah in July 1951 as he entered the Mosque of Omar in Jersusalem, ended today with the naming of his nephew, Crown Prince Hussein - a pupil at top British public school Harrow - as the new King.

The teenaged monarch succeeds his father King Talal, the eldest son and natural heir of Abdullah, who suffers from an incurable schizophrenia which has left him unfit to rule.

A three-man Regency Council will continue to govern while the new King finishes his education. He confirmed his intention to remain at Harrow and plans to attend the British military academy at Sandhurst when his studies are completed.

AUGUST 24

Kenya Curfew Aims To Curb Mau Mau

Alarmed by 'growing unrest and disregard for law and order', the Kenyan government today imposed a stringent curfew order on three districts near the capital Nairobi.

The move is in direct response to the actions of arsonist gangs belonging to the Mau Mau secret society which is dedicated to Kenyan independence from Britain and the expulsion of thousands of white settlers. They have carried out a number of raids to burn down the huts of locals who refuse to take the Mau Mau oath. Membership of the society is most prevalent among the Kikuyu tribe, whose mountain homeland is dominated by European landowners.

AUGUST 6

Arabs Denounce Israel-German Accord

Most people welcomed today's announcement of moves to establish diplomatic relations between West Germany and Israel, a nation founded largely by those who managed to escape Nazi Germany's persecution of Jews. Most, but not all. While many Israeli survivors of the Holocaust express their opposition to any dealings with Germany, the loudest denunciation comes from the Arab League, which continues to deny Israel's existence as a sovereign state and views possible German recognition as a blow to its claim that the region is the rightful homeland of Palestinians.

31 Die In Devon Village Flood

The picturesque village of Lynmouth was left looking - in the words of Housing Minister Harold Macmillan - 'like the road to Ypres' when a freak flood hit a large area pf north Devon today, overflowing rivers and swamping houses with mud, rocks and debris so quickly many had no time to escape.

As troops and relief workers (pictured) worked to help survivors, it became clear that 31 people had perished in Lynmouth and thousands more had been made temporarily homeless in the 250 square-mile region worst hit after more than nine inches of rain fell overnight. Three boy scouts, two girl hikers and a postman were among the dead.

Food supplies and fresh water were sent in by the Red Cross as plans were announced for a national disaster fund launch to help those whose lives have been ruined.

JOHNNIE CRIES ALL THE WAY TO THE TOP!

In many ways he was the most unlikely singer you'd expect to succeed, let alone start his recording career with a single which would outsell everything else released in 1952 or cause teen riots which rivalled anything the bobby-soxers of the 1940s had thrown at Frank Sinatra.

But that's what 25 year old Johnnie Ray did, despite being almost totally deaf since childhood and having a sobbing, shrieking singing style which owed more to the outpourings of bible tent evangelists than it did to the accepted supperclub crooning of the time.

The record which made a bonafide pop star out of the Oregon-born 'Prince of Wails' was *Cry*. Released in October 1951 it raced to the top of the US charts by year-end and took up tenure there into the New Year, being joined in the Top 10 by the follow-up *The Little White Cloud That Cried*. Spot a trend here?

It was a trend which quickly crossed the Atlantic to give Ray a British No 1 through March and April, and begin a fan worship which would continue well past the singer's hit-making sell-by date.

That hysteria reached its peak in 1954 when Ray's raunchy *Such A Night* raised establishment eyebrows and was banned by the BBC, despite being the country's No 1. It was way too raunchy for America, where it was refused airplay from day one and sank without trace.

LABEL SWITCH SIGNALS STAFFORD STARDOM

Although 32 year old Jo Stafford had been a well-established and successful recording artist in the US since 1944, before which she'd worked with bandleader Tommy Dorsey and Frank Sinatra, she hadn't scored an international hit.

Signed to Capitol Records from 1944, in 1951 she opted for a move to Columbia. It proved the smartest thing she'd ever done - in a matter of months she was watching her records become the biggest-selling of her career, and starting to give her hits elsewhere.

The first real biggie was *Shrimp Boats* which was a Top 3 hit in the States in January 1952. The follow-up *A-Round The Corner* went one better, becoming America's No 1 in March and sticking in the British Top 3 from April to August. By the end of 1952 the big-voiced lady from California had notched up further huge hits with *You Belong To Me* (in September) and a

version of Hank Williams' country classic *Jambalaya* (in
October-November).

US NO1 FOR SWEETHEART VERA

The phrase 'auf wiederseh'n' might mean 'so long' in
German, but it was a song called *Auf Wiederseh'n
Sweetheart* which allowed Britain's former Forces
Sweetheart Vera Lynn to say 'hello' to her only
American No 1 this summer.

One of the biggest UK stars of the 40s, thanks to her
wartime hits *We'll Meet Again* and *The White Cliffs of
Dover*, the London-born singer had seen her chart
fortunes slide a little in the early 50s, although her
concert and radio-dates diary remained booked solid.

This year saw that change dramatically. As *Auf
Wiederseh'n Sweetheart* topped the UK lists from June to
October and hit No 1 in the US in July, she also had a
British No1 with the *emotional Yours*.

TEX AND FRANKIE'S HIGH NOON BATTLE

As world cinema-goers gripped their seats and the tension
built (would the townfolk rally behind sheriff Gary
Cooper? would the baddies gun him down?) to make
High Noon one of the biggest movies of 1952, a battle
raged each side of the Atlantic to decide which version of
the film's haunting theme song would be the hit.

In America the showdown was won hands down by
country singer and former movie cowboy star Tex
Ritter, whose original recording of the Dmitri
Tiomkin-Ned Washington song was used by *High
Noon* director Fred Zinnemann to great Oscar-winning
effect.

While Ritter's rendition did fairly well in Britain, the
bigger-voiced and more dramatic reading by Frankie
Laine emerged victorious and was the eventual No 1
between August and October.

*Johnnie Ray the
'Prince of Wails'*

SEPT

Nixon Forced To Deny Fund Charges On TV

SENATOR RICHARD NIXON was tonight forced to make a passionate televised defence of the use he'd made of an $18,000 (£6,000) fund provided by a group of Californian businessman to help pay political expenses in his bid to win the Republican Party's nomination as Vice Presidential candidate.

Accusations of fund abuse are not uncommon in the rough and tumble of American politics, but this was the first time a national candidate had used networked TV to protest his innocence and clear his name.

Clearly emotional but forceful, Nixon said all the fund had been spent on legitimate items, with none going to his family. His wife Pat, he said, did not own a mink - only 'a respectable Republican cloth coat'. Close to tears, he told his audience he would never return one gift which had been made to his six year old daughter Tricia, a cocker spaniel puppy called Checkers (pictured right).

Suspicions that General Eisenhower could drop him as running-mate evaporated as Ike said the broadcast had completely vindicated Nixon. 'As far as I'm concerned, he stands higher than ever before', he told reporters.

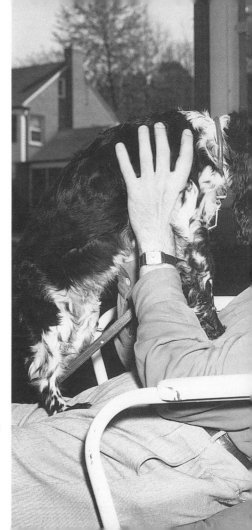

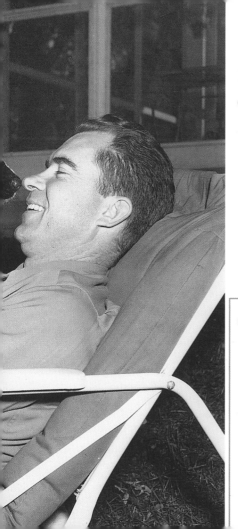

Speed King Cobb Killed

John Cobb, current world land-speed record holder, died today racing his jet-engined speedboat *Crusader* during trials for an attempt on the world water-speed crown.

The accident happened on Loch Ness, Scotland. Cobb, who was 52 years old, had pushed *Crusader* to the 240 mph mark when the craft hit three pressure waves which experts say had built up in front of the prow.

Shocked friends and assistants raced out to where the disintegrated shell of *Crusader* lay on the surface and recovered John Cobb's body from the cockpit.

US Jets Raid Near Russian Border

American jets from the aircraft carriers *Princeton, Boxer* and *Essex* carried out the biggest raid of the Korean War today when they hit North Korean oil and steel plants only 12 miles from the Russian border.

More than 160 planes, protected by cover from Sabre fighters in an area known as 'MiG Alley', took defences at the Musan foundry and Aoji oil refinery by surprise.

The raid was described by Vice Admiral JJ Clark, the 7th Fleet Commander, as 'a sign that we mean business and that we intend fighting hard for our way of life'.

ARRIVALS

Born this month:
1: Manuel Pinero, professional golfer
2: Jimmy Connors, US tennis champion
8: Jeff Miller, cricket player
9: Dave Stewart, UK rock musician, writer, producer (Eurythmics)
12: Gerry Beckly, US folk/rock artist (America)
13: Randy Jones, US pop entertainer (Village People)
19: Nile Rodgers, US pop musician, writer, producer (Chic)
28: Andy Ward, UK rock musician (Camel, Marillion);
Sylvia Kristal, French soft-porn actress (*Emmanuel*)

DEPARTURES

Died this month:
7: Gertrude Lawrence, musical comedy actress
26: George Santayana, Spanish author and philosopher

NEWS IN BRIEF

SEPTEMBER 19

FBI Investigates Chaplin

In an astonishing display of paranoia, FBI chief J Edgar Hoover today set in motion an investigation into the political affiliations of one of the world's best-loved comic actors, British-born Charlie Chaplin.

Chaplin is accused of being a subversive, a catch-all category which can be supported by the flimsiest of evidence, including the unsupported say-so of professional rivals.

Apparently unconcerned by the potentially-damaging situation, on September 23 Charlie returned to London for the first time in 23 years. His arrival was greeted by mass fan hysteria.

SEPTEMBER 30

Labour Turns Left

Britain's socialist Labour Party took a distinct swing to the left today when six out of the seven constituency seats available in an election for the party's policy-making National Executive Committee went to supporters of hardliner Aneurin Bevan. Bevan had resigned his government post as Minister of Labour in April 1951 when Chancellor Hugh Gaitskell introduced prescription charges for spectacles and dentures - a move Bevan considered desecrated Labour's National Health Service ideal of free medical treatment for all.

Among the moderate great and good who lost their NEC power base were Herbert Morrison and Hugh Dalton, both architects of the party's post-war victory over Winston Churchill's Conservatives.

SEPTEMBER 7

Neguib Moves On Suez

Flushed by the success of his ousting of King Farouk, Egypt's new political boss General Neguib initiated moves guaranteed to put him on a heavier collision course with Britain over control of the disputed Suez Canal.

September 7 saw him force Prime Minister Aly Maher - less than two months in office - out of his post, and assume the title and powers for himself.

On September 18 it was learned that the General planned to add a legal arrow to his bow and have the Egyptian parliament nationalize the Canal, so eliminating any British claims on the strategic link between the Mediterranean and the Arabian Gulf.

Jet Crash Kills 26 At Air Show

Twenty-six spectators were killed and more than 60 injured today when a prototype de Havilland 110 jet fighter broke up over Britain's annual Farnborough Air Show. Wreckage showered the 150,000 crowd who'd just watched and heard the jet break the sound barrier, with the worst damage coming as one of the engines ploughed through spectator stands and a car park.

Messages of sympathy for the families of those killed - including 30 year old test pilot John Derry and his 24 year old observer, Anthony Richards - were sent by Queen Elizabeth and Queen Mary. The government announced the immediate creation of an inquiry board to investigate the tragedy.

US Election Promise War Hots Up

American presidential candidates Dwight D Eisenhower and Adlai Stevenson spent some of their campaigning time this month doing the time-honoured thing: making promises about what they'll do if elected.

Described by liberal press and media commentators as an arch-conservative, Republican hopeful Ike told a Chicago meeting on September 5 that he intended to include a black in his cabinet when he moved into The White House.

Democrat Stevenson, condemned as a wishy-washy liberal by conservative writers, did nothing to allay their worst fears. On September 20 he pledged to ensure that blacks enjoyed the same employment rights as whites when he was elected.

OCT

112 Dead In London Train Smash

THE NORTH LONDON Harrow and Wealdstone rail station was likened to a glimpse of hell today after an inter-city express ploughed into the wreckage of two other passenger trains which had collided at the busy commuter stop.

In the second-worst accident of its kind in Britain this century, 112 were killed and more than 200 injured as tons of twisted metal flew through the air to create a 50-feet high pile of debris. More than 40 of those dug out of the wreckage were listed critical by local hospitals.

At 7.31 am, a London-bound commuter train about to leave the station was struck from behind by an express from Perth, Scotland. Seconds later, the third train - travelling north from the city - piled into them to create a tangle of carriages across six tracks which almost demolished the station itself.

American airmen at the scene were among the first to begin pulling frantically at the wreckage as rescue work began. Blood supplies and salvage equipment came in from all over London, as did sympathy messages from Queen Elizabeth and PM Winston Churchill, who ordered a top-level investigation.

Aussie Test For First British A-Bomb

Australia's north-western Monte Bello islands were the site for the successful testing of Britain's first atomic weapon today - witnessed by scientists and servicemen aboard nearby British and Australian warships.

The blast, which created a ragged cloud unlike the now-familiar mushroom of US bombs, was also seen and felt by observers 100 miles away on the mainland. They reported a heavy air pressure pulse which 'smacked' the mainland about four minutes after the flash.

OCTOBER 11

Attlee Slams Labour Left

Accused by right-wingers of 'dithering and doodling', British Labour Party leader Clement Attlee today attacked hard-left firebrand Aneurin Bevan and his supporters for running what he described as 'a party within a party'.

Attlee's outburst followed a further set-back as Labour's national executive, already dominated by Bevanite newcomers *(see September)*, was joined by another two - Richard Crossman and Harold Wilson.

While the Conservative government grinned happily at Attlee's discomfort, he enjoyed a notable victory on October 23 when Labour Members of Parliament approved his NEC motion outlawing unofficial groups in the party. Five days later the Bevan MPs decided to 'suspend' their activities.

Born this month:

2: John Otway, UK rock entertainer/eccentric

5: Harold Faltermeyer, German/US rock arranger/producer

7: Graham Yallop, Australian cricketer

14: Chris Amoo, UK pop singer (The Real Thing)

15: Roscoe Tanner, US tennis player

18: Keith Knudsen, US rock musician (The Doobie Brothers)

29: Arnel Carmichael, US rock musician (Raydio)

31: Bernard Edwards, US pop musician/writer/producer (Chic)

OCTOBER 1

US Infantry Kill Chinese Prisoners

IN ONE OF THE DARKEST chapters of the Korean War, American guards brought in to quell a demonstration by Chinese prisoners of war, opened fire and killed 52 PoWs who'd attacked them with rocks and makeshift clubs.

The tragedy, which happened in a compound on Cheju Island, off the south-west Korean coast, eclipsed a similar clash at the Koje Island camp *(see June)* and led to an international outcry.

It appears that Chinese PoWs had staged the demo to celebrate the third anniversary of the communist takeover of China. Fearing trouble, the camp commander had banned any mass assembly, but prisoners refused to join work parties and began to run amok, waving communist flags and shouting slogans.

When loudspeaker orders to disperse were ignored, two companies of infantry were sent in. Met by a hail of missiles from prisoners barricaded behind the partly-built walls of winter quarters, the soldiers began firing - with devastating results.

OCTOBER 1

The News That Cheers

The British, as everyone knows, love their cuppa. So the cruel rationing of tea inevitably introduced in WWII as more strategically-important cargoes headed in convoy to the British Isles, was just one more thing beleaguered Brits could curse Hitler for. All that ended today, and millions of pieces of china clinked in celebration, as the government announced the end of tea rationing.

OCTOBER 25

UN Rejects Red China

Soviet Russian delegates who stormed out of the UN in January 1950 when the US and Britain vetoed Communist China's first application for membership, have obviously learned that such displays get them and China nowhere.

So they confined their protests to outraged speeches and undisguised anger today when the Mao Tse-Tung regime's third attempt to join the international forum got the same thumbs-down.

Most Western nations continue to support the claim of the Formosan-based Nationalist Chinese government of General Chiang Kai-Shek to represent China's masses in the UN, although many think the mainland communists should also be allowed delegates.

OCTOBER 20

UK Steps Up Mau Mau Clampdown

The British government today signalled a get-tough policy towards the Kenyan Mau Mau terrorist organization which has murdered more than 40 people - including the highly-respected Senior Chief Warahui - in recent weeks.

As Kenyan authorities declared a state of emergency and began a round-up of Mau Mau suspects, men of the Lancashire Fusiliers were flown in from the Suez Canal Zone as a battalion of The King's African Rifles were heading in from Tanganyika. Initially operating only under cover of night, the Mau Mau have begun striking at any time and have acquired guns to supplement their traditional weapon, the knife known as the *panga*.

On October 21, the authorities included Jomo Kenyatta, President of the pro-independence Kenya African Union, in their haul of prisoners. More than 500 other Mau Mau supporters were rounded up by troops on October 30.

MARCH 7
VIV RICHARDS

The islands of the West Indies have produced more than their fair share of cricketing heroes, but few come bigger than Vivian Richards, the brilliant all-rounder born in Antigua this day.

A precocious talent, Viv became a regular member of the West Indian international team while still in his teens, and while his medium-paced bowling was used to advantage by long-time captain Clive Lloyd, it was as a batsman that Richards shattered records in test matches and as a linchpin of the Somerset county side with his good friend and deadly rival, England's Ian Botham.

Viv's first record-book entry came in 1976 when his 291 runs against England at The Oval made him the first player to score more than 1,710 Test runs in a calendar year. In 1985 he made the highest score in England for 36 years with a remarkable 322 in Somerset's win over Warwickshire.

The natural successor to Lloyd when he finally retired as West Indies captain, Richards and Botham left Somerset in 1987, with Richards settling in as a key member of the Glamorgan team. A year later he became the

first West Indies player to score 100 centuries when leading his team against New South Wales in Sydney, Australia.

Viv Richards announced his retirement from first-class cricket in 1994, leaving the international arena with his integrity, decency and brilliance intact and probably impossible to match.

NOVEMBER 17
DAVID EMANUEL

There's no doubt that fashion designer David Emanuel's finest hour came on July 29, 1981 when Lady Diana Spencer emerged from the state coach which had carried her to St. Paul's Cathedral in London for her wedding to HRH Prince Charles. With the world watching, attendants bustled around the new Princess to arrange the magnificent wedding dress designed for her by David and his wife Elizabeth.

Born in South Wales on this day, David Emanuel was fascinated by fashion design from an early age, studied the subject at college and, when he and his wife opened their first London boutique (simply called Emanuel) in the late 1970s, found that the young rich set shared their love of romantic and classically-inspired clothes.

And then came that call from Buckingham Palace....

DECEMBER 29
FLETCHER HENDERSON

One of the most respected pioneers of big-band jazz in the 1920s and 30s, Fletcher Henderson's greatest contribution to music was his skill as an arranger – something the more successful Benny Goodman had every reason to count as an invaluable blessing.

Born in Cuthbert, Georgia in 1898, Henderson was an able pianist who found early work as an accompanist for jazz-blues singers Bessie Smith, Ma Rainey and Alberta Hunter before forming a number of influential bands which included the likes of Louis Armstrong and Benny Carter in their line-ups. Joining the up-and-coming Goodman initially in 1935, Henderson was arranger for many of the self-titled King of Swing's most popular numbers through the next decade. He fronted his own band at New York's Cafe Society Downtown before a stroke ended his playing career in 1950.

Goodman and others helped start a fund to help him, but a number of heart attacks, the last on December 28, 1952, proved too much. Henderson died at Harlem Hospital the next day, mourned by a jazz fraternity which boasted many others for whom he had been a gifted arranger – Count Basie, Jack Hylton and The Dorsey Brothers included.

Ike Sweeps To Victory In US Election

GENERAL DWIGHT D EISENHOWER today experienced the greatest victory of a life packed with wins when he became the new President of the United States of America - his biggest-ever popular vote of over 33 million giving him a 6,500,000 majority over Democrat opponent Adlai Stevenson.

Although that majority was short of the landslide 8,000,000 win of President Roosevelt in 1936, Ike's personal achievement was not reflected by his party as a whole. The Republicans will have a slender majority of one in the Senate and only 10 more in the House of Representatives.

Stevenson's defeat was no disgrace. He polled more votes than any other Democrat candidate in history, with the exception of President Roosevelt in 1936 and 1940. His campaign was run by a devoted army of enthusiastic amateurs, many of whom wept when their man conceded defeat at their Springfield, Illinois HQ.

Ike's popularity is generally viewed by commentators as proof of America's wish for a father figure to lead them through the real horrors of the Korean War and the imagined threats of the East-West Cold War. At President Truman's behest, Ike was to fly to Korea on December 5, even though he will not take up office until January 1953.

Also at that inauguration will be Ike's Vice-President, Californian Senator Richard M. Nixon, the youngest-ever to hold that post at only 36. The highly-publicized charges of fund abuse which clouded his campaign clearly didn't sway voters.

Another newcomer via this election is the 35 year old new Democratic Senator for Massachussetts, John F Kennedy, who upset all poll predictions by seeing off Republican elder statesman Henry Cabot Lodge, the man who masterminded his party's adoption of Eisenhower as presidential candidate.

Devoting the first weeks after his election to picking his cabinet, on November 20 Ike announced that John Foster Dulles was to fill the key role as his Secretary of State.

South African Police Shoot Rioters

The already-explosive South African situation worsened this weekend when police killed 17 Africans in a stone-throwing mob protesting a government ban on strike meetings in East London and Kimberley. A further 39 were wounded.

The death toll rose when it became known that two whites had also been killed in the disturbances - one of them an Irish nun who worked in an East London mission clinic. Sister Aiden, formerly Elsie Quinlan from Cork, was driving near the town when her car was overturned and set ablaze by rioters.

An insurance agent was the other European killed, the victim of a rampaging mob which spilled out of a beer hall in the mining township of Kimberley after a fight broke out among striking miners.

4: Queen Elizabeth opened her first Parliament since becoming monarch

10: A Swedish airliner from Los Angeles became the first passenger plane to fly over the North Pole; UN Secretary General Trygve Lie resigned

11: London: Eneurin Bevan defeated 194-82 by Herbert Morrison in election for Labour Party deputy leadership

12: Iran PM Mossadegh made Britain a new offer to help solve the oil dispute

19: In Vietnam, French forces prepared for an all-out Viet Minh offensive

27: The only Bevanite elected to Attlee's shadow cabinet - Aneurin Bevan

NOVEMBER 18

Kenyatta Accused Of Mau Mau Leadership

KENYA'S BLACK NATIONALIST leader Jomo Kenyatta (pictured right) was today charged with heading the top-secret Mau Mau organization responsible for a widespread murder campaign aimed mostly at the country's white settler ruling class.

Arrested with hundreds of other Mau Mau suspects last month, Kenyatta has been flown to the remote country station of Kapenguria, which has no telephone or rail station. It was there that a District Commissioner officially made the Mau Mau leadership charge.

Married to an English woman, Kenyatta spent most of the war working on a farm in Sussex. He began his active political life in Kenya organizing independent schools for Africans and using Kikuyu tribal pressure groups to agitate for land rights.

Thirty-four Kikuyu schools suspected of Mau Mau sympathies were closed down on November 14, and open rebellion by the Mau Mau in response to Kenyatta's arrest led to the round-up of 2,000 Kikuyu.

NOVEMBER 9

Israel Loses Weizmann

Chaim Weizmann, the first president of the new state of Israel, died today at his home in Tel Aviv, aged 77.

An internationally-renowned chemist, humanitarian and intellectual, Weizmann was an early and leading member of the Zionist movement which proposed and promoted the dream of a Jewish nation in the biblical homeland of Palestine.

Born to poor parents near the Russian town of Pinsk, Weizmann not only lived to see his dream eventually come true, but to become the most natural choice to be Israel's first leader.

NOVEMBER 30

Island Destroyed

A tiny island in the Pacific vanished this month as the US Atomic Energy Commission tested its first hydrogen bomb. The island, part of the Eniwetok Atoll, was the site chosen for the test which a Commission statement issued today said included 'experiments contributing to thermo-nuclear weapons research'.

The term 'thermo-nuclear' is evidence that the device which obliterated the island was an H-bomb. These fuse light atoms, such as hydrogen, together in a thermo-nuclear reaction to create vast amounts of energy. They are made all the more powerful because an atom bomb is used as a 'trigger' to start the fusion reaction.

NOVEMBER 24

Mousetrap An Open-And-Shut Hit

The Mousetrap, thriller writer Agatha Christie's new whodunnit play, opened in London's West End tonight to please critics and baffle audiences as they tried to guess which of the eight characters in a snow-bound house kills during a power cut.

While one reviewer said Miss Christie 'maintains her form', no-one guessed they'd been present at the first night of what was to become the world's longest-running play. Still going after all these years, the first actor to play the inspector who comes calling was a young Richard Attenborough.

DECEMBER 11

Bentley To Hang For Craig's Cop Killing

DEREK BENTLEY, the 19 year old accomplice of Christopher Craig, a 16 year old hoodlum who shot and killed policeman Sidney Miles after a bungled burglary, was sentenced to hang today, even though he had given himself up and had tried to persuade Craig to hand over his weapon before the shooting.

Because of his age, the killer - described by Lord Goddard, the Lord Chief Justice, as 'one of the most dangerous criminals' to stand in the dock of London's Old Bailey Court - escaped the death penalty and was sentenced to be detained at Her Majesty's pleasure.

Bentley's sentence is viewed by many as unjust. Though no-one condones his complicity, the trial evidence proved him to be educationally subnormal and completely dominated by Craig, a vicious gun freak.

There is also doubt about a crucial incident moments before Craig fired nine shots at PC Miles on the roof of a Croydon, south-west London, warehouse. Held by police, Bentley had shouted 'Let him have it, Chris', something his defence team had said was a request for Craig to hand over the gun and surrender.

Although the jury recommended mercy for Bentley, their verdict came at a time when the government had announced plans to clamp down on firearm possession. That, and the fact that the victim was a police officer, led Lord Goddard to the most severe sentence available.

A family petition to the Queen was no more successful than their Appeal Court plea for mercy in January 1953. Derek Bentley was hanged at Wandsworth Prison, London, on January 28.

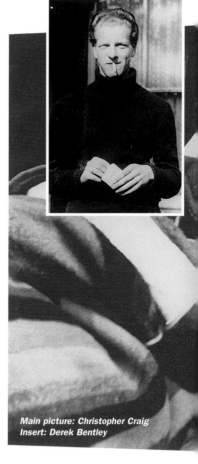

Main picture: Christopher Craig
Insert: Derek Bentley

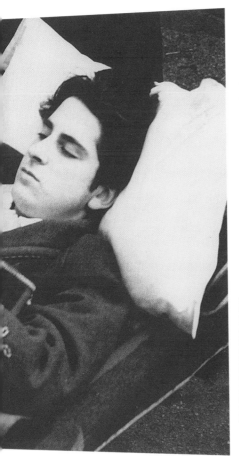

Lord Nuffield And Sugar Ray Retire

This month saw the end of two vastly different though equally-glorious careers which left their respective fields the poorer.

First to announce his departure was Lord Nuffield. The 75 year old industrialist resigned his directorships of The British Motor Company and Morris Motors - operations he had helped steer to international prominence - on December 17. The following day, the sports world was saddened to learn that world middleweight boxing legend Sugar Ray Robinson had decided to call it a day.

One of the most gifted, charismatic and popular fighters of all time, Robinson would return, however. In 1958 he'd win his title back to become an unprecedented five-time champion.

Kiss 'n' Tell Santa Hit

While Gene Autry's perennial saga of Rudolph's red nose popped up to add another few hundred thousand sales to its multi-million status, this year's biggest Yuletide hit on both sides of the Atlantic is *I Saw Mommy Kissing Santa Claus*.
A cute story about a little boy's dismay at catching his mother getting amorous with the guy in the red cloak and wondering what his Dad'll say when he snitches, it gave the previously unknown US singer Billy Boyd his only real hit in an otherwise undistinguished career.

NEWS IN BRIEF

8: In Israel, Itzhak Ben-Zvi succeeded the late Chaim Weizmann as president

10: In Stockholm, Nobel Prizes for Felix Bloch and Edward Purcell (US, Physics), British research chemists Richard Synge and Archer Martin, and American physician Selman Waksman (Medicine). The Literature Prize went to France's François Mauriac.

20: World's worst air tragedy to date when 84 aboard a USAF transport plane died in a Washington State crash

25: The Queen made her first annual Christmas broadcast

27: A car mine killed 10 Muslims in Malaya's worst terrorist outrage

DECEMBER 10

Schweitzer Wins Nobel Peace Prize

Albert Schweitzer, the French intellectual considered by many as a modern saint for his medical and pastoral work with impoverished Africans in the Congo, was today awarded the Nobel Peace Prize in the Norwegian capital Oslo.

The financial windfall will go to help Dr Schweitzer modernize his jungle settlement's hospital facilities.

A noted mathematician, scientist and gifted organist, Albert Schweitzer turned his back on a glittering career to devote his life to helping generations of people for whom he represented their only hope of treatment, food and comfort.

DECEMBER 8

Queen Agrees To TV Crowning

Next June's Coronation of Queen Elizabeth will be broadcast on TV, it was announced today. The BBC have been given permission to cover the pomp and ceremony as the new Queen is acknowledged as head of the United Kingdom of Great Britain and the British Commonwealth, and to sell edited footage of the historical day's events to other countries.

Television has become an international household item since King George VI's coronation and there were some within the BBC who felt the event was too important to be beamed into the world's living rooms like some trivial entertainment.

DECEMBER 17

Row As Ike Consults MacArthur

IT WAS PERHAPS INEVITABLE that America's president-elect should get together with a long-time army buddy to discuss ways in which the Korean War could be ended. The controversy which broke today was caused by Eisenhower's choice of advisor - General Douglas MacArthur, the man fired as Supreme Commander, Far East in April 1951 by President Truman for ignoring orders to keep his opinions to himself, especially the view that the US should expand the conflict by attacking China.

The two WWII veterans met for a working lunch at the New York home of Ike's newly-appointed Secretary of State, John Foster Dulles. Eisenhower had only just returned from a fact-finding visit to Korea and was keen to share his still-fresh impressions with MacArthur.

It was a remarkable political gaffe by the new president, especially as he made public in a press statement what could - and perhaps should - have stayed a private matter.

The statement, which said 'We discussed the problems of peace in Korea and the world in general', gave Democrats the chance to express serious concern and orchestrated outrage at Ike's judgement.

Christine Was Soldier George

Operations to change men into women (and vice versa) are nothing new, but until today and the publication of the current *'American Weekly'* magazine, no transsexual has dared to admit having undergone the treatment.

Truth is, the tall blonde now known as Christine Jorgenson and whose pictures hit US newsstands, was previously called George and had served for two years as a male member of the American Army!

Christine (pictured), who was given $30,000 (£10,000) for telling all, was transformed in the transsexual capital of Copenhagen by six operations and more than 2,000 hormone injections.

YOUR 1952 HOROSCOPE

Unlike most Western horoscope systems which group astrological signs into month-long periods based on the influence of 12 constellations, the Chinese believe that those born in the same year of their calendar share common qualities, traits and weaknesses with one of 12 animals - Rat, Ox, Tiger, Rabbit, Dragon, Snake, Horse, Sheep, Monkey, Rooster, Dog or Pig.

They also allocate the general attributes of five natural elements - Earth, Fire, Metal, Water, Wood - and an overall positive or negative aspect to each sign to summarize its qualities.

If you were born between February 6, 1951 and January 26, 1952, you are a Rabbit. As this book is devoted to the events of 1952, let's take a look at the sign which governs those born between January 27 that year and February 13, 1953 - The Year of The Dragon:

THE DRAGON
JANUARY 27, 1952 - FEBRUARY 13, 1953
ELEMENT: WATER   ASPECT: +

Dragons are mysterious, exotic people who exude sexuality. They are libidinous and very popular with the opposite sex.

Adaptable and accomodating, Dragons fit in with whatever is going on around them. But they are also self-determined and won't submit to being dominated by others, so despite appearing agreeable and adaptable, they can be ferocious and dangerous.

Dragons are essentially powerful people, being kind and generous when allowed to take the lead. They are often found in positions of authority because they prefer to be in charge. It's no coincidence that the Dragon is the symbol of the power and magnificence of the Chinese emperor. Intellectually, Dragons are clever, bright and sharp, though they will throw all logic aside to follow their intuition. Things invariably work out well on these occasions because Dragons also tend to be lucky and land on their feet.

The Dragon is the luckiest of all signs and good fortune follows wherever they go. They also have the Midas touch, so the Year of the Dragon is good for business and money-making schemes. Dragons attract money and generally enjoy financial prosperity. Because of their easy-come attitude to money, Dragons are generous and hardly ever broke.

Dragons are also gifted creatures with an especially-original turn of mind. They can be ingenious and resourceful, picking themselves up when they're down, whether physically, psychologically or materially to make fabulous come-backs. They never say die, never accept defeat and can be guaranteed to live to fight another day. Temperamentally hot-headed and quickly irritated, Dragons will give as good as they get when angered, and do not display great sensitivity. They can be hyper-critical if things aren't quite right, or not up to their expectations.

Generally, Dragons don't have to work at being liked - they are glamorous and magical, can light up gloomy moments and express a huge need to be loved.

FAMOUS DRAGONS

Lord Jeffrey Archer
Author/politician

Geoffrey Boycott
English cricket player/TV commentator

Jimmy Connors
International tennis champion

Sir Edward Heath
British politician/yachtsman

Kirk Douglas
Film actor

HRH Prince Edward
Theatrical producer

Sir Yehudi Menuhin
Violinist/teacher

Zandra Rhodes
Fashion designer

Ringo Starr
Drummer with the Beatles/actor